REFLECT

Meaning; think deeply or carefully about...

I_____ pledge to complete this

Journal and reflect on it in a years time to note any changes of progress

or failures and also my efforts.

Dedication

This was written to allow us to look back on the years and experiences we've had and realise where we were and where we are now.

I have added established and personal quotes.

Are you where you want to be in life, if not, why? What changes occurred?

Maybe we are still on our path...

It was created to encourage and help us in our life journey, despite our past. Also, to understand why we are the way we are and to reassure us that it is ok, but we can make changes if we wish.

We make more changes than we realise!

My mum and daughter have been patiently waiting for me to complete this diary and are always encouraging me so, I dedicate this to them for their patience and support.

.

I love and appreciate you and hope that I have inspired you to grow and always acknowledge your root no matter how bent it may be because it holds the answers to your future...

Contents

Introduction

Young adults this is mainly for you but recommended to all ages over 18 due to the content. I created this diary to help you to recognise your behaviour, make changes, release emotions and sustain your mental health. For you to grow, look back on where you were and look forward to where you are going. It is ideal for those that feel there is no one you can talk to, no one understands you or you have difficulty opening up.

Please realise that nothing good can come out of you bottling up your emotions, because anger and festering emotions only reproduce uncontrollably and most often negatively.

Use this book to verbalise your emotions and feelings and then reflect on your circumstances later and evaluate your journey. See your progresses and downfalls and continue to make positive changes, even the smallest of steps are effective.

I will speak of topics that you may relate to and give you the opportunity to release your experiences and the effects they have had on your life good or bad.

Sometimes we do not see where our behaviour arises from until we speak or read our own experience. You will identify how you can make changes, I want for you to counsel and heal yourself, where possible and be able to identify if it is best you seek help, where unable to help yourself.

It's your journal. Make it as detailed as you wish for it to be, but it will have no effect if it is untruthful, adapted or even worse, unused!

So, let's begin…

IN
THE
BEGINNING...

Childhood; My childhood was simple but nice. I have a great Mother who didn't have much to give me but made up for it with plenty of love. We would dance, sing, swim and laugh a lot. I had a step-dad who I didn't have the best relationship with but it also wasn't the worst, I just knew that he didn't accept me because I wasn't his. This made me uncomfortable, made my mum unhappy and eventually the relationship ended. My Mother and I always had a close relationship, and I never felt the need to keep secrets from her. We moved away from everything and everyone we knew to begin a new life, but this was not an easy outcome and we experienced family feuds, my step-dad attacked my mum in front of me. My mum and her sister fell out for years because she had told him where we were living; knowing that he had threatened her life.

Having that bond with my mum that I still have, made up for the fact that my Dad wasn't a daily part of raising me but we did have some contact. I missed not having my Dad around on a regular basis and I hated the fact that when I would stay with him, he would always be out so I spent most of those weekends with his girlfriend or alone. Luckily his girlfriend and I got on well, so, it was ok, but I felt as though he wasn't interested in me and didn't understand why he bothered collecting me if he didn't want to spend time with me.

"*Your childhood forms the root of the adult you desire to grow into. If broken from the root, can give you a desire to fight and heal or to lose all faith and strength, there are only ever two destinations".*

How was your childhood, is your earliest memory a good or bad one?

What do you think a child needs consistently?

What did you appreciate that you received consistently in your childhood?

What do you desire consistently as an adult?

A child deserves mental stability and freedom to feel without fear of judgement.

- Were you encouraged to speak freely with boundaries?
- Were you praised for your achievements and encouraged to succeed?
- Did you feel wanted and cherished or unwanted and under- valued?

How has this impacted your life?

Notes

_____

_____

_____

_____

_____

_____

_____

_____

_____

_____

_____

_____

_____

_____

_____

_____

_____

_____

Write a letter to your younger self

Dearest _____

_____

_____

_____

_____

_____

_____

_____

_____

_____

_____

_____

_____

Signed _____

Draw your own version of your family

Upbringing; Were you raised in care or by someone other than your natural parent, did you have an absent parent or two, how did this make you feel, does it still impact your life?

You can be raised by a natural parent and receive less love than you would from a carer.

A person can have a child, but it doesn't warrant them a parent! What was your experience emotionally?

"The broken root again if placed in water will mend and grow,if weak and not supported will damage but if strong will outgrow all breakage and blossom".

- Did your upbringing cause damage or happiness?
- Were you given attention?
- Were you able to express your feeling

Fill in the facial expressions to reflect your upbringing.

Siblings; I was an only child for my mother and was the youngest of my step-brothers and sisters and then later on came my two half- brothers (a term we do not use). With this I never had to fight for attention or felt left out, are you a middle child, one of many in a big family or a single child too?
Were, or are you spoilt with attention or competing for a glimpse? How does this make you feel?

"Having siblings can prepare you for competition later on in life"

- Do you have a good relationship with your siblings?
- Has it got better or worse since becoming an adult?
- Are there big age gaps between you?
- Has this had an impact on your relationship?
- Is there or has there ever been rivalry?
- Has this caused conflict?

Notes

Early relationships; I had a lot of friends and my mum was someone that children loved to be around because she was a fun mum, she would take me and my friends and my cousins swimming, park, cinema or McDonalds and it was always great being out with her as she would make up silly songs with us and join in our stupid dances but also leave us to our privacy to be children.

Having no siblings, my relationship with my friends and cousins were very special. How was yours...?

"Relationships from young teach you how to relate as an adult, it is a skill that is innate or learned behaviour".

- Did you have a close friend, or pet?
- What were your hobbies, did they keep you entertained in another world?
- Did you first learn to love by bonding with your pet?
- Did you struggle to make friends, were you a loner?
- What are your earliest memories of friendship?

Notes

Primary; School was the best for me. In my school days it was fun, playing kiss chase and feeling free. There are good and bad memories here.

I remember being dragged down the stairs by my hair when I was around 8 by my head teacher.

I remember my first boyfriend and the first boy to attack me at every opportunity because he wanted me to be his girlfriend, yes mate, I remember!

I also remember my friend being abused by her stepdad and people bullying a particular girl because she was smelly.

My worst memory is finding out that one of my childhood boyfriends had committed suicide because of his abusive relationship with his dad and this was all in primary school!

I was always confided in by friends and it hasn't stopped.
How were your primary years?

"School years should be your best years, unfortunately, not every child has the best experience"

- Do you remember primary school and any major events that took place?
- Did you enjoy attending?
- Did you have a favourite teacher or a not so nice one?
- What impact did your teachers have on your school life?
- Were you liked by peers and teachers?

Notes

Parents; Growing up with separated parents is not an ideal life-style.

However, I have no idea if it would have been beneficial to me if they had stayed together? I guess I'll never know. We always desire what we cannot have and often do not appreciate what we do have!

My relationship with my dad is now strong but has taken many years to get to this point.

My relationship with my Mum has never changed she has always been there for me. How is your Maternal/Paternal relationship?

"Parenting can affect your whole life in a negative or positive way, there is no handbook for the best parent but we have a choice of how we choose to parent our own if and when that time arises".

Parents have such a humungous responsibility.
If we get it wrong, we can spoil not only our child's
life but also who he/she engages with in the future.

We parent by instinct and hope.
If you turned out ok, then you will mirror your
own upbringing, if not, you usually try to go the
opposite way.

Some get caught in the pattern and continue the
trauma because they haven't released their own
traumas yet, which brings fourth the opportunity
to spiral downwards.

• Do you feel your parents got it wrong, or that
you have. If so, why?

• What would you do differently and how
Would it shape things in your eyes?

• As an adult can you see how some situations
came about or certain decisions were made?

Notes

Family; My family relationships are lacking. I was always close to my cousins that I grew with on my Mum's side of the family but on my dad's side of the family we are not often in touch but if we do visit, it isn't noticeable or uncomfortable.

I have two very different relationships with both sides of my family. I am more comfortable with my Mums side and make more of an effort to be in touch with them because I feel the connection and the love is reciprocated with some, I suppose it's just familiarity.

However, my dad's side does not make as much effort and I feel it's basically 'out of sight out of mind', which is unfortunate because the love is still there. There are all types of characters in every family, which ones and why, have had the most or least impact on your life?

"Reciprocation is important; it shows value and encourages longevity."

Family by blood doesn't mean that they are chosen. Sometimes gentle boundaries need setting.
We are all human and need forgiveness but also to forgive.
The weight of the trauma that we carry holding on to things can materialize into forms of ill health. If it is too heavy to bear, let go. Sometimes you must take the lead and break barriers for your own sanity.
If family life is good, then that's wonderful and most likely because someone had the best 'top down' leadership approach.

- Are your friends your chosen family?
- Do you keep healthy relationships?

Notes

Write a letter of forgiveness to a family member/parent for anything that you still hold, that is still holding you back. Release it!

Dearest _____

_____

_____

_____

_____

_____

_____

_____

_____

_____

_____

_____

_____

Singed _____

You may need another...

Dearest _____

_____

_____

_____

_____

_____

_____

_____

_____

_____

_____

_____

_____

_____

Singed _____

And another...

Dearest _____

_____

_____

_____

_____

_____

_____

_____

_____

_____

_____

_____

_____

Singed _____

Did you let go of the emotions that you have been carrying?
If carried out correctly, you should feel lighter.
How do you feel?

Did you feel protected and loved?

Were you missing that presence?

Has your relationship changed as an adult?

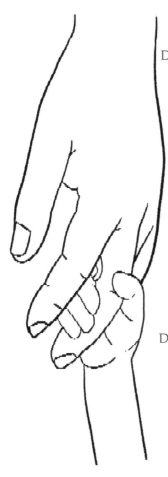

Did you lack guidance?

Do you feel abandoned or let down?

Did you lose a parent, how has it changed you?

Do you have good memories or bad ones?

When are you most affected, do you notice a pattern?

EXPERIENCES...

Real friendships; Leaving my home town of London and moving away from all of my friends and family was very difficult as I had no choice! I made some very good friends over the years but realise that very few of those friendships stay strong due to growing apart and having limited time for socialising. Especially when you become a mother/father, wife/husband, studying, employed/juggling etc which is a shame as other things take priority, and less effort is made both ways.

From having a lot of friends as a youth, currently, my real friends are no more than a handful and are all long-term friends. It is a shame, that we wish we had paid more attention to our relationships with others when it is too late! How were your relationships with siblings and friends and how are they now? Did you move around? Are/were you in a gang or the head of one where your loyalty was due to your circumstances?

"Long-term friendships that can stand the test of timeand close relations show commitment, balance and loyalty on both sides".

Not all friendships/relationships turn out to be what you expected…

- Do you hold some real ride or die friends?
- Do you have those ones that are only there for a good time?
- Can you call your friends over when your lonely and they turn up with a drink or food or nothing, but they still show?
- Are your friends only around you when you're up and when your down they're nowhere to be found?
- Have you or your closest friend done something unforgiveable that cannot be repaired?

Which friend/s do you call when you are extremely happy or sad? And why?

Do they call on you? Why/why not?

Notes

Secondary; I was slightly bullied in secondary for my first year, by one girl who was best friends with my close friend and didn't like how close we were. This stopped immediately when my Godmother, collected me one day and questioned her actions in a language that she understood; after that it was as if I had imagined the whole experience!
How were your secondary school experiences, were you bullied, were you the bully or the teachers' pet? Did you wag school? Were you excluded?

"This is where you are supposed to come into your own as a young adult and you begin experiencing anxiety and weird changes and emotions and you don't want to share those feelings, so you struggle alone."

Were you a confident or shy teen?

Did you have good experiences such as school trips?

Did you have braces/bad acne and had to grow into
yourself or were you simply superfly?

These crucial teen years open new doors...
The pressure of relationships, hormones, emotions, peers, exams, and then career choices.
It's the fine line between being a child and a pre-adult. *'Shit gets real here'...*

• How did you handle these changes?

• Some people struggle to shift from here to adulthood.

• How has it impacted you?

Notes

Accidents; My first major accident was at the age of three when I was electrocuted and almost died. I still have the scars on my hand to remind me of DANGER!!!!!! I also broke my arm in a park when I decided I would swing so high that I went over the swing bar and flew out of the seat. Luckily, I was with friends who ran to my home and called my mum who then called an ambulance whilst legging it down the road toward me because they told her I was dead, I was unconscious!

Thankfully, these are the only serious accidents I've incurred so far.

The latter one taught me not to push boundaries too far. I did watch a school friend of mine get hit by a car whilst riding his bike near the school and that image has stayed with me and always reminded me that danger just like death is not biased to age, race, size or sex. What is your experience of accidents?

"Accidents put fear into us by opening our eyes to danger, it doesn't mean we must stop living but becautious in our decision making".

- How serious was your accident or have you been lucky?
- Has an accident impacted your health long-term or changed the course of your career?
- Have you caused an accident? How has this impacted your mental health?
- Be honest with yourself and seek help if needed

Notes

Loss; I have had many losses but they have not affected me deeply as in they were not immediate friends or family. However, they shocked me, for example, a murder of a relative when I was 9, elderly relatives, an aunt to cancer at 17, an uncle to alcohol, another aunt to cancer, followed by a close friends' child aged 10. Amongst my dog who ran away, rabbit, budgerigar's, Guinea- pigs and hamster which affected me as a child as they were my first personal loss experiences to name a few. What losses have you had and how did they affect you?

"Death teaches us to value others and ourselves.It should also encourage us to live and not just exist".

Deep longing for someone will only become lesser with acceptance. Losing something or someone is one of the hardest pains to bear, give yourself time to feel the many mixed emotions that loss brings.
Not allowing yourself to feel can bring on other complications.
Be honest with yourself and seek help if needed, bottling up always has a negative knock-on effect.

Remember that only you know, how you feel.
Sometimes you need to share that pain.

- What losses have you had and how did you overcome them or have you not?

- Would you advise someone close to you to handle their loss in the same way?

- How would you advise someone to deal with their loss following your own experience and why?

How did you handle your grief?

Do you have any regrets on how you dealt with it?

Notes

Image; As a teen I went through a stage of acne, it wasn't the worst in the world but even one pimple is the worst thing in the world at a certain age and it had a negative effect on how I saw myself especially when theywere commented on. I felt 'ugly' despite peoples opposite opinions. I was also chubby but comfortable in my skin until the doctor called me overweight! This one comment was all I needed to hear to feel fat and spotty, signifying 'ugly'!
How has your image affected you and your confidence?

"It only takes one negative tongue to lower your self-esteem. Why is it that when a thousand tongues are encouraging you the only voice that's clear among them is the single hurtful one?"

- Has your image changed?
- Are you content or unsatisfied?
- Do you see what others see?
- What are your best/worst bits?
- Do you base your image off of others' opinions or social medias expectations?
- Do you have self-love? If not, why?

Notes

Draw an image of your younger self

CIRCUMSTANCES

Social life; Mine is naff!! Due to my own actions. I have many friends and enjoy the company of others but only in small doses, I'm too homely which means I'm content. I'm happy with a hot chocolate, a blanket and a good movie. I think I over- did it growing up and now that I am settled withmy family life I don't have much time for a social life. This is apain when I watch movies like 'girls trip' I feel like 'yeaaah, I wanna go on a girlie vacay (vacation) but wait, I haven't beenin touch with anyone for over a year, so how is this gonna work out?' I wish I could manage both social life and familycommitments. I must work on this! How is your social life?

"Balance is important, too much of one thing is good for nobody. Everything in moderation is key"

- Do you take time out to socialise with others?
- A healthy balance is needed for good mental health
- What is your routine, has it been interrupted or affected and why/how?
- How did the lockdown affect your social life?
- Do you have any exciting plans or new year goals to enhance Your social life?

Notes

Financial status; My family wasn't wealthy but I was clean, fed, clothed and well loved. I didn't have the latest designer clothing but I was happy regardless and unfazed by labels. What was/is your household income, not in figures but status, were you financially comfortable, struggling or wealthy? How did this affect you?

"We are not rich by what we possess but what we can do without"

Immanuel Kant

- How important is your financial state to you?
- Did you have a wealthy upbringing?
- Did your parents struggle?
- Are you mean/generous?
- How has this impacted you and your financial beliefs/goals?

Notes

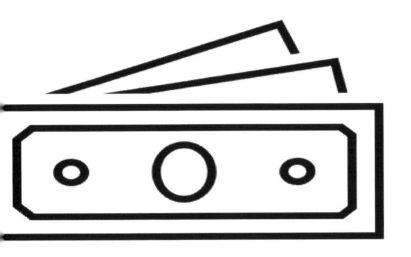

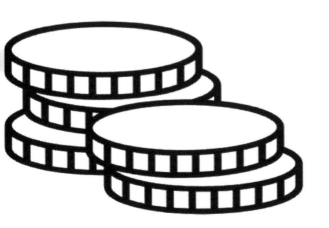

Opportunity; As an Adult I am not quite where I want to be in life, I believe I expected to achieve so much more although I have more than I expected, if that makes sense. I believe circumstances changed my destiny and now I see different opportunities than I did before. Where are you now; have you met you ambition of job role; are you working toward your dream job? Are you confused in career choice or are you making money in the wrong way? Do you have a record and are struggling to get on your feet? Feel like there are no opportunities for you?

"Don't live in regret over missed opportunities, for if you do, you will miss even more."
— Charbel Tadros

- Has life been fair to you?
- Does your life feel like you missed out on something?
- Do you want to make changes?

  It's important not to dwell on missed opportunities

Notes

What is on the other side of the door for you, are you ready to walk through?

Career; I studied hard all of my academic life and took my degree In Criminal justice and Psychology but ended up teaching and neither of those fields seem to be enough for me, I am still seeking that role unbeknown to me that fulfils me as an adult. Who are you today? Have you become who you thought you would? I knew I was destined for motherhood and a career yet there is so much more for me to achieve, some of which I am still learning myself. How about you…

"Allow opportunities so they won't become missed opportunities."
— *Franklin Gillette*

- Do you love what you do?
- fire you working your way towards your passion?
- Do you have failed opportunities or much progression?
- fire you confused about which way to go in your career?

Notes

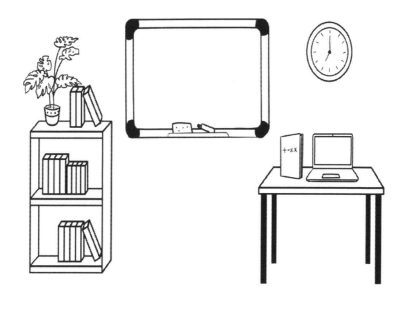

Advice; I think if I was to advise my younger self I would choose my teen years and I would say;

"focus, don't be afraid of living, stop holding back, ignore the negativity and gravitate to the positive influences".

As for now I would say to stop settling and that it's ok to put yourself and your needs first sometimes (if you don't, who else will?) What advice would you give to your youngerself? What advice would you give to yourself now looking inon your life?

Advice given should not always be taken, it is advisory for a reason. Be cautious of who you take advise from and always make your own choices.

- What is the best advice you have received and the worst?
- What advice would you give to yourself on reflection?

Notes

Memories; Growing up, my worst memory was watching my mum and step-dad struggle with a knife.

My best memories were the times spent with my best friends just simply chilling…

What are your best and worst memories?

"Don't you wish you couldtake a single childhood memory and blow it up intoa bubble and live inside it forever?"
— *Sarah Addison Allen, Lost Lake*

"The greater a child's terror, and the earlier it is experienced, the harder it becomes to develop a strong and healthy sense of self."
— *Nathaniel Branden, Six Pillars of Self-Esteem*

Good memories can bring peace and happiness. Bad memories can lower our mood and lead to depression and anxiety.

We often remember negative memories over positive ones. Memories can be a reminder to not repeat negative patterns.

Do you have reoccurring good or bad memories of anything and how do they make you feel?

- Do you shut out painful memories or do you allow them to take place and deal with them?

- Do you change your memories to suit your comfort?

- Do you sometimes have memories that cause an outburst of laughter or tears?

- Are you battling a reoccurring memory, if so, have you realized why?

Notes

Lasting friendships; During my teens, I had many friends. Friends that brought me happiness and laughter.

I am still in touch with a few of them today, still melancholy over our past. Reminiscing on events from yesterday. Life has brought us all in different directions/ locations.

Friendships that I thought would never end, did! Those I never thought would last, did! I look at my children's friendships today and they are different, they are based mostly on the phone and social media. My friendships were tangible and therefore to me, more personal and real.

Words exchanged in person cannot be taken in the wrong light as you are present to explain through expression or orally. However, words on text or social media cannot be rectified in the instance so easily before being circulated or misread. We partied, travelled, walked for miles, ate cheap food and played. Life was at its peak. As an adult, I cannot say the same. I have many acquaintances; however, my true friendships are limited.

This may be down to many factors, such as; wisdom, time, family, work life, distance, balance, trust, knowledge, commitments, change, growing apart, I could go on. I believe mine is down to; commitment, wisdom, knowledge and time. I am no longer carefree and have commitments to fulfil, I have learned things about myself and certain friends that I believe will not suit as a friendship any longer and there is never the time to maintain regular communication or meetings which causes distance over time.

"You will attract friends that reflect your environment and circumstance at that time, if when those

circumstances/environment change the friendship is still there with the same energy and commitment, It's a 'true friendship".MD

We are almost halfway through! What have you recognized about yourself so far regarding any patterns, behaviours, moods etc

1

2

3

4

5

6

- How are your friendships? Are they long lasting, do you commit equally?
- Friendships keep us healthy and happy.
- Being able to maintain long friendships displays commitment, and a person's self-security. Friendships are the basis of healthy relationships. Great friendships can fill the gap of family.
- Do you remember your first friendship? What was it that you liked about it and the other person?
- Do you attract the same type of friends as you always did?
- Do you find it difficult to make friends?
- Do you shy away from friends, if so, why and how does it make you feel?

Notes

School/College/Uni effect; How did you feel about school in general? I didn't have the best school experience with staff but made amazing friends, friends that I unfortunately have not maintainedbut have held onto the memories. There was one teacher that I remember gave me encouragement and showed belief in me but isn't it always the way... the one teacher that makes time for you, never stays! I can't remember her name but Thank you Mrs Millonaise (I think)?

Otherwise, school was not what it should have been. It was mainly a power trip for most teachers, the support and care was often missing. However, I enjoyed learning as an adultand continued to study everything I had any interest in. How did/does school make you feel?How has it impacted your life?

"You can drag my body to school but my spirit refuses to go."

Bill Watterson, The Essential Calvin and Hobbes

School has a lifelong impact.

- Did you struggle academically or socially?
- Did you excel or were you left behind needing support and unnoticed?
- Do you have traumas from school or great memories and experiences?
- Did school prepare you for the 'big wide world'?
- Was it necessary in your eyes?
- Was university the right choice for you?

Notes

Stress; When I was younger my mum used to say that I knew nothing about stress and my Dad would say that there was no such thing as stress! I KNOW that they both understand what it is today! Life is a total different ball game now and stress is hitting people from a much younger age now. Stress now begins at primary school, if it hadn't already started at home. It then follows into all of the stages of life that we cover and it basically doesn't end. The most common stresses among us range from bills to relationships and sickness. The whole world of humanity is experiencing some form of stress, unfortunately stress can also impact your mental and physical health. So, try to find some happiness or peace in everything you do.

Stay active, meditate, laugh, play, communicate, dance swim and most of all pick your battles as a wise woman once told me!

EVERYONE HAS THE ABILITY TO INCREASE RESILIENCE TO STRESS. IT REQUIRES HARD WORK AND DEDICATION, BUT OVER TIME, YOU CAN EQUIP YOURSELF TO HANDLE WHATEVER LIFE THROWS YOUR WAY WITHOUT ADVERSE EFFECTS TO YOUR HEALTH. TRAINING YOUR BRAIN TO MANAGE STRESS WONT JUST AFFECT THE QUALITY OF YOUR LIFE, BUT PERHAPS EVEN THE LENGTH OF IT.

AMY MORIN

How do you relieve your stress?

What 3 things stress you the most?

1

2

3

Why do these things get to you so deeply?

How can you change the way you react to these things?

Notes

Envy; As you get older and certain opportunities come your way, you then begin to notice that some friends that you thought were true friends begin to change and become slowly unrecognisable. This is where you begin to let go of certain people and you then attract a new type of friend that fits with your current lifestyle. What are your experiences?

"Change can be a positive experience. Sometimes we need to clear out negativity and embrace change in order to be happy".
MD

- Do you struggle with envying others?
- Where does it stem from?
- Do you feel dissatisfied in your life?
- How can you change this negative behaviour?
- How do you feel when someone close to you is doing really well in life?
- Are you competitive or inspired by others' achievements?

Notes

Love; My first relationship was at the tender age of 6. I ran around the playground being chased by a friend who declared his love for me. 30+ years later, it would appear that he meant what he said. I didn't take him seriously then or now and from his own admissions, it hurt him. I guess I was just young! However, that isn't justifiable for him and I understand that now. I then went on to meet another friend in another primary school who never declared his love but his actions were just as deep as the previous one, he would ask my mum if he could take me on a date and despite being laughed at, he would be persistent in showing his loyalty. I then had teen love and that's where my heartache began or maybe my boomerang for not seeing what my first love experiences had felt. It was a painful experience; I had a crush on someone for two whole years who I walked past on a daily basis and did not have the bottle to even look at him when he passed me. He would say hello and my lips would become entangled in my cheeks, it made no sense.

Later on, I would meet someone who would ask me to be his girlfriend and we would meet in the local park with our friends and innocently kiss and hold hands.

I felt like I was a small person acting older at this tender age of 14.

That lasted for a minor month but felt like ages. Then after a few more of those mini relationships I endured a real serious relationship which brought all sorts of experiences, cheating, abuse, anger, love, pregnancy etc.

How were your love experiences? Are you a lovebird or heartbreaker, proud or jealous with your partner?

"Love is an uncontrollable emotion that can be beautiful, painful or both"

- Are you scared of love, if so, why?
- Do you fall in love easily?
- Have you never had it?
- What does love mean to you?
- Is/has someone abused your love?

Notes

Sex; I wasn't sexually active early and this was my

Choice. I made plans to wait until marriage.

Unfortunately,it didn't go the way I foresaw it,

and my first experience wasn't pleasurable either.

Are you a virgin? There's nothing wrong with

waiting for it tofeel right, in fact that's the way it

should be! For most females there is a lot to consider

emotionallyfor your first time, you want it to be

special and there's nothing wrong with that.

Males rarely connect their hearts to the act of sex.

Did/do you question your sexuality? How was your

first experience? Are you comfortable now?

"When you really love somebody, you can wait"

- Brandy Norwood

Sex produces oxytocin and endorphins which improve your mood.

Soul ties are created during this time.

Your body is your temple so be choosy with who you share it with.

- Are you selective with your sexual partners?
- Do you enjoy intimacy?
- Was your first experience a good one?
- Are you a virgin?
- What does sex mean to you? Is it an act of commitment or simply fun?
- Do you feel safe in your intimacy?

Notes

Motherhood; Motherhood has been a wonderful, amazing, stressful, scary, confusing, worrying roller coaster of emotions and I would not change it for the world. It is the best experience of my life. It's the only thing I feel I'm confident in, at least 90% of the time. I learned from my mother and if I didn't have that amazing role model. I don't know if I'd be the Mum I am today!

Are your children in care? Or with family?

Are you struggling?

"A mother's body remembers her babies- the folds of soft flesh, the softly furred scalp against her nose. Each child has it's own entreaties to body and soul."

— *Barbara Kingsolver*

Motherhood impacts us all differently.

- Are you a mother or wish to be?
- Are you frightened of taking that step?
- Are your children in care or raised by a family member?
- Is motherhood taxing on your mental health or does it fulfil a hole in your life?
- Has it changed your life, how?
- Were you almost a mother?
- Are you a mother to someone else's child?

Notes

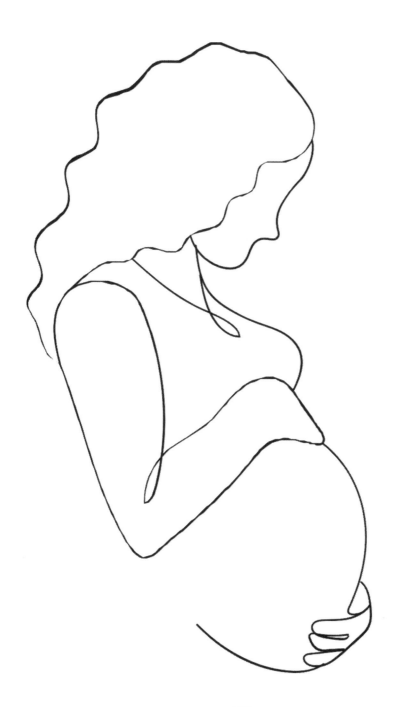

Fatherhood; My Dad has always said that he regretted not being there for me due to the relationship breakdown. Many dads have difficulty maintaining healthy relationships with their children mainly due to parents allowing emotions to overrule what's best for the child/ren.

There are many reasons for breakdowns, but it is important to be consistent and also to seek help if needed, to make sure you are the best possible father and an amicable co-parent for the interest of the child/children.

What does it mean to you? Do you see your child/ren? Are you repeating a pattern, or have you changed a cycle? Do you know what you're doing? Do you need help?

"Every father should remember one day his son will follow his example not his advice "

- Charles Kettering

- What type of father are you?
- Do you desire to be a father or do you not?
- Do you have son/daughter, has it changed you as a man?
- What type of father did you have or did you not have one?
- How has this impacted your life?

Notes

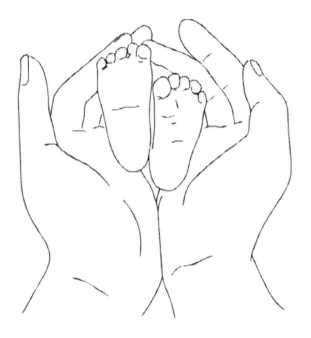

Commitment; Although relationships were valuable to me and still are, I maintain a zero tolerance attitude. I wasnot prepared to stay with anyone that disrespected me, and I wasn't a push- over. I had friends who would settle in disappointing situations, lowering theirself-worth and still to this day. I tried tomake a difference in my attitude as I got older and became a woman. It was necessary for mother-hood and preparation for marriage. This doesn't mean I put up with disrespect it just means that I realise how difficult relationships can be and that it takes commitment and 50/50 effort and respect.

**"Persistence. Perfection. Patience. Power. Prioritize your passion.
It keeps you sane."**

Criss Jami, Killosophy

Fear of commitment and lack of trust can cause breakdowns.
Fear and anxiety can come from lack of trust or abandonment.

- What do you feel comfortable committing to, work, friends, parenting?
- Are short term affairs easier to commit to?
  o Why is this?
- Where does your fear or anxiety stem from?
- What do you fear is the worst that can happen if you ignore the fear, and is it bigger than the risk?

Notes

Adult relationships; This is a whole new dimension. This was where commitments were expected, hearts were broken and lives created. My first serious relationship was forjust under three years and it was totally unexpected, it was fun andexciting because he was wild and unpredictable but in the end that same wild and predictable nature is what tore us apart and broke my heart. This was a lesson that was very valuable but also turned into a great friendship maybe because that's all it should ever have been. Sometimes we meet people and mix up our emotions, such as believing were in love when it is simple infatuation orloving someone as a friend and perceiving it as a relationship. Love hurts and unfortunately, you only learn by experience. How was your experience?

"Sometimes life sends us people who don't love us enough, to remind us of what we're worthy of".

Mandy Hale

The 5 A's of an adult relationship are;

- Attention
- Acceptance
- Appreciation
- Affection
- Allowing

Do these apply in your relationship?

Are you in an unhealthy (abusive) relationship?
If so, seek help, as scary as it may seem. Be bold!
Are you single? If so, what do you desire, from whom and why?

Notes

Pregnancy; The sick feeling, not knowing what to expect. What is good pain, what is abnormal pain? The hormonal emotions, the physical changes and the brains preparation for mother/fatherhood. The baby arrives and your whole perception of life changes, questioning what this means, how do you do it, are you doing it right? How much you love and want to protect him/her forever. On the flipside it may not have been the best experience and you may wish it would all just go away. How did/do you feel?

"The fear of your body being taken over by a brand-new life just waiting to meet and depend on you" MD

- Do you struggle to conceive? Do you get pregnant as soon as he looks at you?
- How does this affect you, being able to or not?
- Does your partner want children and you are not sure?
- Do you suffer with issues that can hinder fertilization, such as endometriosis, cystic fibrosis or other?
- Do you simply not want children?

  This is not a crime as many believe, it is a life -time commitment that should be made without pressure.

  Pregnancy can be one of the hardest things to complete and it is just the beginning… Once baby arrives a part of you leaves, there is so much that isn't shared on this topic, what is your story?

- How difficult is it for you as a man to support your partner through pregnancy and how do you feel?

Notes

Pregnancy Loss; Did you wish to continue the course of Pregnancy or decide to terminate? Maybe you had a miscarriage? Whatever your experience, how did the loss affect you? Was it what you wanted or has it had a lasting effect on your emotional state? Do you battle with your emotions struggling to understand why it happened or if you did the right thing?

"When you left, I lost a part of me" MD

Losing a baby can cause depression, PTSD and other psychological symptoms along with the fear of another pregnancy possibly ending with the same result.

This is confusing for both parents and can put strain on a relationship even if you had to make a choice, It is never forgotten no matter how many children you may go on to have.

- Have you or your partner experienced this loss?
- Did it make or break the relationship?
- Have you gone on to have another, if so, did it cause anxiety for you in the process?
- Did/do you blame yourself, if so. why?
- Has it stopped you from having more children?
- Do you forgive yourself?

Notes

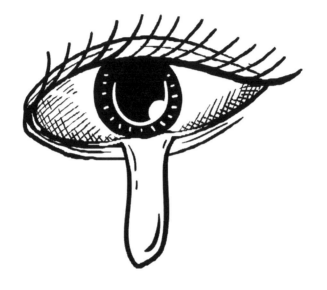

IMPACTS...

Influences; My up-bringing was happy even amongst the turmoil I experienced. No, 'Cosby show' or 'Waltons' family household yet I had the best mother who did all she could in her circumstances to give me the most love and happiness that she could despite not knowing that love herself as a child. My uncle was the perfect father figure in my eyes as a child until I grew up and saw that 'all that glitters isn't gold'. What did life look like for you as a guide to parenting, what/who were your influences? Were they positive or negative? Who did you look up to and who did you never want to be anything like?

" Think twice before you speak, because your words and influence will plant the seed of either success or failure in the mind of another".
Napoleon Hill

- Are you an influencer if so, what kind; parental, powerful, negative?
- Who was/is your biggest influencer and how?
- Are they still as inspiring as you once believed?

Notes

Regrets; I like to say, we should have no regrets because everything happens for a reason and sometimes a season, but I'm aware its not so easy to feel that way, when you're in your situation. However, if I had to choose something; my biggest regret is not moving back to London where I grew up, to raise my children around their family. My biggest fault was having treated certain people too nicely, I've since grown! What do you regret and why? What fault do you own that you have or are trying to change?

"There are no regrets in life, just lessons"

Jennifer Aniston

Regret can lead to self-criticism, sleepless nights, anxiety and more…

There are always more roads to choose that can still get you back on route.

We must also learn to accept that some things are simply meant to be.

- Is your regret your own fault or was it out of your control?
- Can you change your regret or learn to accept it and find some positive in the outcome?
- Do you see the lesson in your regret?
- Can you avoid a similar occurrence in the future or have you already?

Notes

_____

_____

_____

_____

_____

_____

_____

_____

_____

_____

_____

_____

_____

_____

_____

_____

_____

_____

Biggest achievements; Mine is gaining my degree at a pressing time in my life, during a sickly pregnancy and other dramas at the time. I also believe that my persistence to never give up is what got me through it. I hope I have passed that gene on to my children. What are you most proud of? (Don't you dare leave this space blank because it isn't a competition, your achievement can be so small, either way it is a barrier that you have overcome, so spill…)

"Success is not obtained overnight. It comes in installments; you get a little bit today, a little bit tomorrow until the whole package is given out. The day you procrastinate, you lose that day's success."

— *Israelmore Ayivor*

We often focus on where we are not and what we do not have.

Every achievement is a step closer to whichever direction you are heading in.

- What are your biggest/ smallest accomplishments?
- What are you working at to achieve still?
- Do you disregard certain achievements or value each one?
- What has prevented you from achieving your goals?
- Who has encouraged and motivated you to succeed?

Notes

Changes; I would change the fact that I allowed the opposite sex to choose me for their partners because it was what they wanted, it would have saved us all a little less heartache! I wish I'd have had the confidence to follow my dreams and found ways to make them work rather than being put off by all of the things that were in the way. What would you change, what do you wish you had fought for?

"And the day came when the risk to remain tight in a bud was more painful than the risk it took to blossom."
— *Anais Nin*

Coming away from what you know and into the unknown, stepping out of your comfort zone can be challenging. Change is unavoidable but not always negative.

- What changes have worked out for the best?
- What do you struggle to change?
- Who have you tried to change?
- Has your life changed to quickly or in a way that you never expected?

Notes

PRESENT...

Now; What needs to change 'now' for you? What are You doing now that needs to stop or start and why? What effect is it having on your life, on your loved ones, your work, your health, your social life, your finances, let's be honest?

"Out of your vulnerabilities will become your strength."
— Sigmund Freud

We measure against time and some things cannot be controlled or measured. Time can be your friend.

- Have you set some goals, created a vision board?
- Are you happy with where you are in life?

Look back at some of your answers and recognize your areas of improvement and where you can make changes, can you identify and give yourself small, achievable targets?

Notes

Choices; What effects are your life choices having On you, are you happy with the choices you make? What was the last important decision you had to make? Was it the right choice now that you reflect on it? If not, why and if yes, why? My last important decision was do I let my daughter go on holiday with her friends or not? I'm glad I chose to let her go because she had a great time. I didn't worry because of the sensible child I raised, and it allowed her to live her best life which she continues to do.

"It's only after you've stepped outside your comfortzone that you begin to change, grow, and transform."
— Roy Tennett

Don't be pressured…

Take your time to feel and think about the right choice for you and no one else.

- Are you indecisive?
- Do you feel as though your choices have been taken away from you? Are you afraid to make your own choices, why?
- Has a bad choice back-fired in the past?

Notes

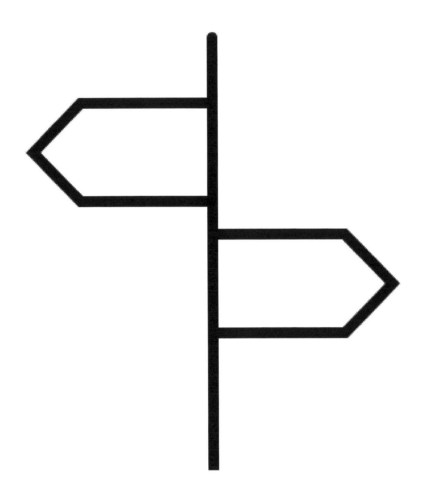

Emotions; How do you deal with your feelings, moods, anger? Do you have someone to confide in or do you bottle and blow?

Were you raised to be silent or have freedom of speech? Are you confident to interact or shy to talk? Can you cry or is that a struggle?

Are you showing signs of depression or suffering with any other emotional trials?

"The best and most beautiful things in the world cannot be seen or even touched. They must be felt with the heart"
—Helen Keller

Talk to someone, spend time with others and ask for help if you know you need it!

Recognise your symptoms and act, don't wait until it's too late and unstoppable or begins to affect your loved ones.

Allow yourself to feel your emotions, don't halt them to be strong, it takes strength to feel, process and fix yourself too.

- How were you taught to deal with your emotions?
- How do you deal with your emotions?
- Are your emotions causing you stress?

Notes

Reflect; looking back can you identify why certain events have turned out the way they have? It's now time for you to reflect on yourself and identify where some issues have risen from and how you can set small goals to make big changes to your life! Once you have set them, I would advise that you return to this book in a years' time and reflect on your circumstances…

"It is never too late to make a change and taking so much-needed alone time for yourself to reflect is not selfish."
— Nyki Mack

Forgotten childhood trauma signs;

- Low self-esteem
- Relationship problems
- Chronic illness
- Inability to cope with change
- Mood swings
- Struggling to act like an adult

Do you relate to any of the above, can you think of where it stems from and re-direct it?

Can you look at your behaviours or reactions and remember why they were held back or forced forward?

Do you see an inherited pattern forming or a development of a character that you no longer need or want in your life?

Notes

145 Try this activity for 5 days

What are you proud of yourself for today?	
What inspired you today?	
What challenges did you overcome today?	
What are you grateful for?	

What are you proud of yourself for today?	
What inspired you today?	
What challenges did you overcome today?	
What are you grateful for?	

What are you proud of yourself for today?	
What inspired you today?	
What challenges did you overcome today?	
What are you grateful for?	

What are you proud of yourself for today?	
What inspired you today?	
What challenges did you overcome today?	
What are you grateful for?	

What are you proud of yourself for today?	
What inspired you today?	
What challenges did you overcome today?	
What are you grateful for?	

Self- Evaluation

- What have you discovered about yourself and patterns or traumas? Does anything make sense now that you are able to reflect on your past and behaviours?
- What changes do you feel you should make?
- What/who do you need to make peace with to move forward? What/who do you need to let go of?
- Who is your biggest advocate?
- What do you need now to allow yourself that time to let go and breathe?

Websites/Links for support and advice

https://www.nhs.uk/conditions/stress-anxiety-depression/mental-health-helplines/

https://www.nhs.uk/conditions/miscarriage/afterwards/

https://www.miscarriageassociation.org.uk/your-feelings/

https://www.prospects.ac.uk/careers-advice

https://nationalcareersservice.direct.gov.uk/

https://www.nspcc.org.uk/preventing-abuse/child-abuse-and-/child-sexual-abuse/

http://www.gangsline.com/

https://www.mentalhealth.org.uk/a-to-z/a/anxiety

https://www.mentalhealth.org.uk/

https://www.nhs.uk/live-well/sexual-health/

https://www.pregnancy.com/

https://www.parents.com/parenting/

https://www.nhs.uk/conditions/Stillbirth/

http://www.understandingchildhood.net/

https://teens.webmd.com/features/teen-dating#1
https://www.victimsupport.org.uk/crime-info/types-crime/domestic-abuse

Printed in Great Britain
by Amazon

41181895R00128